FAREWELL CLUTTER, HELLO PRODUCTIVITY!

Declutter and organise your workspace to maximise your productivity

Written by Bénédicte Palluat de Besset

Translated by Jessica Foster

Coaching 50MINUTES.com

FAREWELL CLUTTER, HELLO PRODUCTIVITY!

- **Issue:** how can I put and keep my things in order and thus improve my productivity?
- **Uses:** tidying and sorting allows us to save time in our everyday actions, but also to free up space in our minds that we can then dedicate to working.
- **Context:** time management, project management, organisation at work.
- **FAQs:**
    - Is getting organised a waste of time?
    - Why does tidying help productivity?
    - When is a good time to get started?
    - What do I do when tidying is made necessary by an external event or factor?
    - How should I structure my to-do lists?
    - What does good organisation involve?
    - Does tidying mean throwing away?
    - What are the sensible tools to have for optimal tidiness?

While some people have been unable to imagine sleeping in a room that is not perfectly tidy since childhood, others live in a constant state of untidiness that does not seem to bother them.

The ability to get organised is more or less a natural faculty; but even if we are relatively enthusiastic about tidiness, at some point in our lives it often becomes necessary to structure our space. In a professional environment in particular, there is nothing worse than a messy desk to make you feel overwhelmed and as if you can no longer get on top of things! Tidying and sorting allows you to make your work and living spaces healthier, and to clear them out so that you can be more organised and thus save time.

But when tidying becomes necessary for ourselves or others, where do we start? How do we get motivated? What methods do we use? What tricks should we implement to keep on track?

CONVERTING A CHAOTIC LIFE TO A TIDY LIFE: THE BASICS

You might feel a sense of admiration for your neat and organised peers. You envy your colleague's impeccably tidy desk every evening, without managing to do the same with yours. Sometimes, you reassure yourself by saying that you have no time to get organised, as you have far too many important things to do. Mistake! Taking the time to think and organise your space depending on its requirements and needs later saves you a huge amount of time in your day-to-day life.

When the time for New Year's Resolutions rears its head, you always write "tidy up" in your top ten priorities. But very soon, faced with the enormity of your mess and lacking effective methods, you get discouraged and end up eventually abandoning this ambitious yet helpful plan.

GETTING MOTIVATED

Sometimes an external factor gives you motivation: the arrival of a new colleague, a longer break from work, moving house. Sometimes, it is also the result of personal awareness – yet another hour wasted trying to find that elusive document, and you decide that it's time to tidy up.

Archivists often say that a poorly-filed document is a lost document. Indeed, you may well have a wealth of information and interesting sources in your office, but if you cannot use them for lack of knowing where they are, they are not particularly useful. Sorting allows you to take an inventory and get rid of useless things. It is a great opportunity to create space and take back control of your room.

Make a list of all the things you never have time to do and/or all the projects you have been dreaming of starting which, for now, remain outstanding. With all the time and energy you will save no longer having to try out three different pens before finding one that works, and not opening four files before finally locating the piece of paper you need, you will be able to get started on many new activities.

Once you have tidied and reclaimed your workspace, you will certainly enjoy being there more. Given how much time you spend in your office, it is worth feeling comfortable there!

SET REALISTIC TARGETS

Starting a basic tidy-up requires you to be motivated and to stay that way for a short while! It is a real project, which requires you to set realistic goals, according to your requirements and needs.

The first thing to do is to list everything that needs to be sorted (the desk, the pile of paper left by your predecessor, the blue cupboard, etc.). Next, set priorities for everything on the list, then set a frequency, as often as possible, and a deadline for finishing every step of the process. For example, give yourself twenty minutes a day before leaving the office. Remember that a private office and an open-plan workspace are not organised in the same way; just like a bachelor pad is not arranged in the same way as a house with three children in it! The expectations are different and the level of demand is not comparable.

PRACTICAL METHODS FOR EVERY SPACE

Tidying your desk

This is certainly the first space to tidy. Firstly, it is generally quite simple to get a desk back in order (keeping it that way can be more difficult, but we will suggest some ways of doing that!), which is very motivational. Additionally, as well as being very noticeable, it is a change that you will immediately appreciate on a daily basis.

To do this, sit behind your desk and look at all the things on it so that you can sort them into their proper place.

- Throw away everything that is broken or unusable.
- Give away or set aside the supplies you have two of, or that you no longer have use for.
- Send or forward the documents that do not concern you to the correct recipient, having first informed them by email that these documents will be turning up (date of arrival, number, reason for sending them, etc.).
- Sort everything you do not use on a daily basis into your desk drawers. To do this, consider dividing your space up. Having boxes and/or cases in your desk drawers allows you to make optimum and sensible use of the space. Put your paper clips in an old box for business cards, your stapler and matching staples (it is possible!) in a pencil case, and so on. These tricks will help you to have everything to

they are a head of department who must delegate many tasks to different people in their team. In that case, all they have to do is forward each of your emails to the individuals concerned.

Create a complete automatic signature: Name/Surname/ Department – Title/Address/Phone number/Email. If you are easy to identify and to reach, you will increase your chances of receiving a quick reply. Equally, if your message requires a reply, indicate the date by which you would like to hear from the recipient, leaving a small margin for error in your favour.

Write a message of absence in advance, in which you will only need to update your dates of absence. This will save you precious time on the evening you leave. When you come back from your holiday, open your emails from the most recent to the oldest, not the other way around. The people who have been waiting ten days for a reply can wait one more day. Recent emails, however, are either reminders, in which case they require action; or they contain extra information or changes to instructions and it is therefore useless to waste time with the previous messages; or they are new requests, and you will have responded quickly.

Finally, the last piece of advice we can give you is to know when to log out of your email inbox. The notification message that appears on your computer screen the second a new message arrives is not the best way to be efficient, far from it. Checking your messages regularly, every hour or every two hours, is of course important, but stopping whatever you are doing as soon as an email arrives is counterproductive. It is essential to relearn how to concentrate on one sole activity by disregarding your colleagues for a relatively long time (25-30 minutes minimum). This is the best way of truly getting stuck into your work, concentrating, developing ideas and having time for quality reflection.

Keeping on top of your diary

Writing your meetings, lunches, seminars and other appointments in your diary allows you to give your brain a rest and to avoid forgetting half of your commitments. A diary is also a tool which allows you to assess how much time you are spending on things. When we are trying to become more productive, re-reading it is often informative.

Some swear only by technology to manage their schedules, others would not let go of their paper diaries for the world. Everyone should do what they prefer, as long as the format is suited to their needs. On the other hand, whether your timetable is electronic or on paper, a few simple rules will allow you to make the most of it.

- A meeting obviously has a start time, but stating a finishing time as well as an agenda is a good way of avoiding disappointments.
- Whether for professional or personal appointments, write a phone number next to the name of the person you are meeting. If they are still not there after 15 minutes, it will be a relief to be able to call them; equally, you will have a contact number to hand if unexpected circumstances mean you are late. Write the address of your meeting point in the time slot for the appointment

too: this will avoid last minute searching in case you are rushed when leaving.

ORGANISING YOUR HOUSE TO OPTIMISE YOUR WORK

Once your professional space has been tidied up, you will find it increasingly difficult to deal with chaos at home. Besides, you will soon realise that this lack of organisation of your home and your personal life is making you waste a lot of time at the office. How many times have you been the last one to arrive at a 9am meeting because, in the morning, nothing was working at home? The bill you urgently needed to pay, the shirt you had to iron before leaving, or your youngest child's coat that you found only after hunting through the pile of dirty laundry for 15 minutes...and just like that, you are already late and under pressure before you have even started your day at work.

A few rules

In the morning, every minute is precious! Well-monitored organisation will allow you to arrive at the office in good time and therefore to get started on your professional files in peace before the rush of your colleagues' arrival and the incessant stream up and down the corridors.

To do this, you need to take a few preparatory measures, starting the evening before: lay out your clothes for the next day, lay the table for breakfast, get your bags ready.

Arranging your house logically not only allows you to save time on a daily basis, but also to delegate better, which is important if you have to entrust your house to a third party for housework or looking after the children. When all the 'side jobs' (maintenance, housework, childcare, etc.) are under control, it will be possible for you to focus on one task and therefore to be productive to finish the project you are working on, organise a team meeting or fully concentrate on your yearly appraisal.

EXTRA INFORMATION

Generally speaking, organise your home so that you can avoid running back and forth as much as possible. For example, so that you don't have to go all the way to the second floor to brush your teeth after breakfast on the ground floor, put a toothbrush and toothpaste next to the kitchen sink.

Set more or less frequent intervals, depending on the task, for dealing with papers, getting on top of your ironing, starting the dishwasher, washing machine, etc., planning meals and doing the grocery shopping. Of course, this sets up a routine, but this regularity saves time and frees our minds so that we can be more efficient. Check your post every day, just like you do at work, and buy a file in which you can put the papers that need sorting and dealing with, ready for the day you have selected for dealing with all your papers. Do not forget to bin adverts, leaflets and other flyers that invade our letterboxes and clutter up our tables.

Involve your children

Harmoniously reconciling professional and family life is many parents' dream! It is true that the presence of children, especially when they are young, is often very time-consuming and requires a particularly well-oiled organisation so that the parents can continue to fully carry out their professional duties.

But in the face of this challenge, your best ally is actually your beloved offspring! As long as you take the time to make them independent and to set a few simple rules, even very young children (as young as three!) are capable of doing many things alone, such as tidying their rooms, making their beds, getting dressed by themselves, clearing the table, etc. To help them with this, make sure that bin bags are easily accessible for them, opt for a duvet instead of traditional bedcovers, get their clothes ready the night before, but above all, accept that they will sometimes make small mistakes! If your child is in charge of the tidiness and organisation of their environment, that means fewer things for you to do, but it also means that they will learn habits that are essential to healthy, balanced family life. You will be much less stressed and less worn out with anxiety if you leave a tidy house, and especially if this tidiness is the result of everyone's participation!

STAYING ORGANISED

Now that you have done all your sorting and your living and working spaces are perfectly organised, the challenge is to keep it on track! Doing a little every day is the best solution. You need tidiness and order to become a reflex, a state of mind, so that you realise the extent to which it is a self-fulfilling cycle.

In short, tidy as you go along, as this will stop chaos from ensuing! When you create a document, immediately sort it into the correct folder; when you receive an email that does not concern you, forward it immediately; put your stapler away as soon as you have finished using it; throw used envelopes away as soon as you open the letter, etc. The same goes for the little habits to acquire which will help you to avoid spending five or ten minutes clearing up before you leave the office. And regularly do a total clear-out: sorting out your pen pot, taking stock of your famous temporary storage spaces, etc.

The final point to bear in mind is that you must periodically ask yourself if your organisation is still relevant to what you are doing. Your needs and expectations evolve and you need to adapt your organisation to these changes. Bernard Calvet (French businessman, born in 1935) said that even the most perfect organisation needs to be changed around every ten years or so. So don't worry, that gives you plenty of time to think about it!

TOP TIPS

- Stop procrastinating and take action! You will definitely have to do all this much talked about tidying at some point. Tomorrow you will only find another excuse not to get started on it, so you might as well start immediately!
- Make to-do lists. Writing down your list of things to do on paper helps you to set objectives, rank them according to importance and make them happen. This is both a way of taking action and a way of clearing your mind. And think of the satisfaction you'll get from crossing something off the list!
- Analyse your needs and requirements to set realistic rules. Implementing effective organisation requires questioning ourselves and considering what is not working in the current model. Starting from this observation, you will find satisfying and productive organisational solutions.
- Think about your space in terms of limiting movement around it. This rule works just as well for the office as it does for your home: the aim is to facilitate frequent access to various things, so keep the most useful items within reach.
- Find a relevant organisation system that helps you to delegate easily. To cope with an overwhelming amount of work or a temporary absence, you may need to delegate tasks to someone outside your department. To make their arrival and your return easier, and to keep up a satisfactory quality of work, it is important for this new recruit to be able to find their place in your organisation

system without too much difficulty.

- Open your post as you go along. Throw away useless things, forward misdirected mail, and immediately read or temporarily store post that requires action on your part. Regularly sort through the papers you have dealt with.
- Create schedules to organise activities that happen regularly: the team meeting every other Thursday; the weekly sorting of your professional file on Friday afternoon and of your personal file on Friday evening; lunch with your counterparts from other departments every first Monday of the month, etc.
- Focus on one activity for a set amount of time. To do this, close your door, ignore your email inbox and set up your phone to go straight to voicemail.

<u>THINGS TO AVOID</u>

If you have your own office, avoid leaving your door open permanently; close it without feeling awkward. If it is urgent or very important, your colleagues can knock. On the other hand, having your door closed prevents inane conversation. Some people might say that this attitude does not create a good atmosphere... this might be true, but having a constantly open door encourages unplanned meetings and requests. The breaks for coffee and lunch are there to create this much talked about bond between co-workers.

- Learn to anticipate. Start by never putting off what you

can do right now. Thereafter, try your best to make pro-gress. If you know that in a fortnight there will be a rush at the office, organise yourself so that you have as little as possible to do at home on those days. If you are at risk of being requested to do something the next time your new boss comes in, make sure that your files are tidy and your work tools are immediately available to you.
- Keep tidying as you go along. To do this, nothing more is required than to do a little each day.

FAQS

IS GETTING ORGANISED A WASTE OF TIME?

Of course not! It is simply an investment. Getting organised actually requires a fair bit of advance planning, questioning yourself, figuring out what is not working, analysing your needs and priorities and listing the actions to carry out to achieve realistic, sensible and effective organisation. But aside from that, you will save an incredible amount of time!

WHY DOES TIDYING HELP PRODUCTIVITY?

When you organise your space, you actually tidy up on two levels. First of all, physically: by organising your things, you will know where they are, so you will not waste any more time looking for them. But in particular, by organising, you are taking stock, analysing and conceptualising, and this state of affairs helps you to better organise your mind and, in doing so, improve concentration and efficiency.

WHEN IS A GOOD TIME TO GET STARTED?

Straight away! On a more serious note, it is not worth starting a spring clean or enormous organisation project while you are in the busiest period of the year. As we have previously said, tidying, sorting and organising requires a few hours to begin with. You need to get started when you are motivated and are ready to spend some time and energy on it.

WHAT DO I DO WHEN TIDYING IS MADE NECESSARY BY AN EXTERNAL EVENT OR FACTOR?

Sometimes, moving house, a colleague leaving or the arrival of our firstborn child compels us to have a large-scale tidy-up. The first thing to do is perhaps to welcome this new requirement as a fantastic opportunity! The second step consists of establishing a reverse schedule so that your new organisation is operational when you move, when your team gets smaller or when you go on maternity leave. Final tip: start by reorganising the spaces that will be most useful to you, as this will motivate you for what comes after.

HOW SHOULD I STRUCTURE MY TO-DO LISTS?

There are two ways to approach this:

- List the actions to carry out in order of priority, which is linked to the importance of the tasks and their degree of urgency;
- When you are not particularly rushed and you have tasks of similar importance in front of you, it's up to you to decide: for some of them, the best method is to list and deal with the elements to manage by starting with the ones that you find the most boring. You will be much more efficient, as you will be keen to move to a more exciting activity. Not to mention, having a tedious task behind you frees your mind to concentrate on other things. For others, however, it is more effective to start

with a motivational task to warm up, but to then spend time on at least one boring task per day.

WHAT DOES GOOD ORGANISATION INVOLVE?

Whether in the office or at home, for organisation to be productive, it must meet your current needs, be feasible in the long term (which does not mean that it will never change) and follow logic that is comprehensible to others (in order to facilitate delegation).

DOES TIDYING MEAN THROWING AWAY?

Of course! Tidying means clearing out so that you do not simply move the chaos around. You surely have unusable office supplies and out-of-date documents in your desk drawers, and your computer is surely full of obsolete IT tools and double copies of files. As for your email inbox, it undoubtedly contains emails that, while they might be from colleagues, are not necessarily professional. Getting rid of these is a liberating action!

WHAT ARE THE SENSIBLE TOOLS TO HAVE FOR OPTIMAL TIDINESS?

You will obviously have to analyse what you need, but ideally you should keep things simple. Envelope folders with straps or elastic bands and sub-sections are efficient tools for sorting through your papers. On your desk, a vertical partitioned folder works very well as temporary storage space.

OVER TO YOU

PLAN OF ATTACK TO PUT AN END TO CHAOS AT WORK

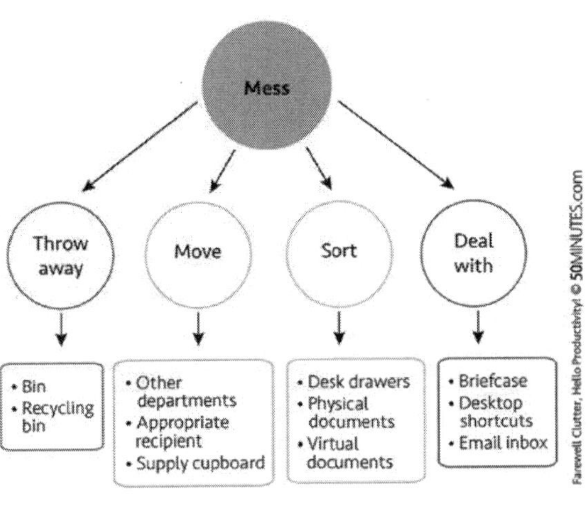

PLAN OF ATTACK TO KEEP IT UP

Daily schedule

Make a chart which reviews, for every day of the month, the actions that you have to undertake to keep your space in order. And every day, cross off an action as soon as you have done it!

	Tidy desk	Tidy computer desktop	Check email inbox	Open post	Look at timetable for the next day
1					
2					
3					
4					
5					
6					
7					
8					
9					
10					
11					
12					
13					
14					
15					

	Tidy desk	Tidy computer desktop	Check email inbox	Open post	Look at timetable for the next day
16					
17					
18					
19					
20					
21					
22					
23					
24					
25					
26					
27					
28					
29					
30					
31					

Weekly schedule

As well as your daily schedule, make yourself a list of the basic, slightly more time-consuming actions to do regularly but not daily (once a week or once a month, etc.).

	Check contents of temporary storage space	Spend 30 minutes on basic work: clearing out files, improving computer tools or creating draft documents	Tidy a small space from top to bottom
Monday			
Tuesday			
Wednesday			
Thursday			
Friday			

We want to hear from you!
Leave a comment on your online library
and share your favourite books on social media!

FURTHER READING

BIBLIOGRAPHY

- Arce, C. (2015) Rangement de bureau : 5 conseils (vraiment utiles) de Marie Kondo. *Terrafemina*. [Online]. March 2015. [Accessed 14 March 2016]. Available from: <http://www.terrafemina.com/article/rangement-de-bureau-5-conseils-vraiment-utiles-de-marie-kondo_a266832/1>
- Bureau, N. (2008) *L'art de l'organisation*. Québec: Broquet.
- Roland, O. (2008) 3 étapes pour un bureau clair en permanence. *Habitudes Zen*. [Online]. September 2008. [Accessed 14 March 2016]. Available from: <http://www.habitudes-zen.fr/2008/3-tapes-pour-un-bureau-clair-en-permanence/>

ADDITIONAL SOURCES

- Kondo, M. (2011) *The Life-Changing Magic of Tidying*. London: Ebury.

www.50minutes.com

Ebook EAN: 9782806289025

Paperback EAN: 9782806289032

Legal Deposit: D/2016/12603/734

Cover: © Primento

Digital conception by Primento, the digital partner of publishers.

Made in the USA
Monee, IL
07 July 2026